I0415492

Collected Critical Essays

Wading through the Nonsense

Art, Education, Governing, Finance & Health Care

Mark Ruhala

Mr. Ruhala is available for lectures, seminars and workshops.
He can be contacted at: mcruhala@msn.com
Also visit him at: **www.RuhalaCenter.com**

ISBN-13:
978-1491264652

ISBN-10:
1491264659

Dedication

This collection of essays is dedicated to
the free thinkers in my life that taught me to stand alone:

My Mother, Julia Mae Joseph Ruhala
My mystery teacher, Dr. Brugh Joy
My wife, Celina Matos Ruhala

ACKNOWLEDGMENTS

Life herself is the teacher.

CONTENTS

The Education of Children and
The Education of an Artist

MAIN STREAM EDUCATION

Main stream education is set in a hierarchical power structure, starting with the federal government and the state, working down to the superintendent and the board, working down to the principal and assistants, down to the teachers and aides, down to the students. At each and every step, one has a set limit of power over others. At no place is there egalitarianism. Hence the lack of dignity students like myself feel in their second class status which offers lack of power in decision making or constructing one's own life.

All the work in schools is based on a reward system. You do not have to really learn to be rewarded, as is evident with many athletes' education, or when alumni pull strings, or when wealthy persons use their money to buy positions, and by the cheating scandals that expose all the cheating that goes on that we do not know about. The rewarding of gold stars, grades, awards, scholarships, and degrees becomes the driving motivating source for students to climb the ladder. And schools have an intense pressure to give these carrots out because their funding and reputation is contingent upon it. In this system, cheating is common place and rampant, I have been hearing about it from my students for twenty years.

In our schools the pressure to conform, which is the antithesis of development, is felt by every single student, and felt intensely. Independent thinking is not encouraged. To stand out is dangerous and its punishment starts with simple humiliation and progresses to sanctioned suspension and expelling or worse still, violent verbal and physical abuse, which is sometimes fatal. Our schools have one way to educate and are rigid without a diverse set of educational approaches that would serve other kinds of learners. Most learning takes place from memorizing information from text books not from having real life experiences. This kind of learning is short-term and only rarely gets into long-term memory – just think about how much you learned in school that you have forgotten. I have heard many parents shy away from home-schooling because they are afraid they couldn't teach past fourth grade math. Advanced math becomes part of the short-term knowledge we learned that for most of us, is not necessary or relevant to our adult lives. Even if we developed those neural networks back then, we have lost them from lack of use. Our brains require that we use it or lose it.

The homogeneous setting of same age students from similar economic backgrounds, often racially segregated, does not reflect our world or community, and rarely opens minds by offering new experiences and new kinds of people.

The cutting of arts programs has kept the arts out of the core curriculum and relegated their stature to an unnecessary elective part of education. Often students take these courses only because it is an easy class from which to get a good grade. I have had two students here, both academically well suited, who wanted to create an independent study program to work more in depth in the arts. One student's principal could not even comprehend the idea, and the other students' guidance counselor pressured the student to take more classes and stay in school so the district would receive more money.

Often we have really good teachers and administrators whose hands are tied behind their backs by the system. This system advances some students and holds back others. And the artist, who lives and breathes life from a sensuous, aesthetic, irrational, intuitive, processed oriented outlook, will never succeed in this kind of environment.

A contemporary ideal of our educational system pushes students to become involved in many extra-curricular activities. This idea, I believe, has two basic thoughts behind it which we have accepted without thinking. (Much has been written about how we accept rules, laws, regulations and restrictions without thinking. This too, I believe comes from our conformist ways of educating and the loss of independent thinking.) We are led to believe that the more we are exposed to, the better. I hear parents constantly tell me how important it is for their children to be involved in many activities because it is good for the children to be exposed to as much as possible. This, like so much of our ways of living has to do with the economic paradigm we live in: as long as the economy grows, it is good! And just as we have not yet woken up to the fact that all this growth is destroying the quality of our lives through stressing our environment and ourselves, we have not seen that the doing of so much activity is too destroying the quality of our lives by stressing our families, our relationships, and ourselves.

The other basic thought behind this ideal to do everything is that it will help you get into a better college and help with admissions. Although in some cases this might be true depending on what one is doing, the stress caused by the overextension of activities will null and void any benefit that is to be had. Even summers, our break from the academic setting which could be full of trying new things, are often taken up by school in the hopes of attending better colleges and taking less college classes through the intensive reading required for many AP classes. And now, some educators are asking that teenagers stay in school two more years before going to college because they simply cannot learn all the information there is to know in twelve years. If you want to see the extreme of this kind of planning for the future and forgetting about the present, look at the private pre-schools in New York City. Families pay $40,000 a year for pre-schools that have long waiting lists, just so their kids will have a jump start to their academic careers. Those kids, like the kids here who are being pushed, either by themselves, their parents, or the systems, are not happy when they are stressed and they are clear about it.

THE NEGATIVE EFFECTS OF OVEREXTENDING ONESELF

When we stop and consider what is going on it is clear why these kids are not happy and how damaging this stress is to our physical, emotional, and spiritual being. In short it goes like this: First we overextend ourselves, taking on more than we can manage, committing to too much, with the thought that we must do these things or that "we can handle it", not seeing the pitfalls about to devour us. Soon we realize we are buried, which brings stress, then we begin to anticipate the stress which creates more stress, and soon we are not really doing much of anything very well. Then the people in our lives who are expecting more from us get frustrated or disappointed, and we compound this with our own frustration and disappointment, and especially the need for it to go away so we can enjoy our lives again. By now, our bodies have dealt with stress on many different levels: usually starting with emotional, moving into physical, and on to spiritual and psychological. The stress response in our bodies is a specific physiological process designed by nature to protect us short-term from dangers. It releases very important hormones and chemicals, corticoids that activate our muscles, respiratory system, and cardiovascular systems for action. In the short-term, we can live with this. In the long-term, as with chronic stress, we create hypertension that stresses our systems into dis-ease. Our immune system stops functioning well, and the body begins to break down. We usually are so worried at this point that we do not sleep well, if we get enough sleep in the first place, which most teenagers do not. And sleep is a most important time for the body to repair and regenerate itself. We all know what it is to be sleep deprived and we all know the ill effects it has on us. It is said that 70 to 90% of Americans have a stress-related disorder and end up in a health care facility thereof. And yet we continue to push ourselves and our children with little regard to these ill effects, all in the name of getting into a better college or simply because we need more. The idea of more, in and of itself is a costly frame of mind, more will never be satisfied, it will never end.

One solution is to appreciate what we have, and to want only what we need. We will have less activity and fewer toys, and we will have more health and more happiness.

AN EXPERIENCE OF EXCELLENCE

On the flip side of this picture is the experience of excellence in one activity. To experience excellence is to have true accomplishment; no reward necessary. The inner life that accompanies the experience of excellence is one of exaltation; no person on the outside can offer this. No grade or award can come close to the true inner feeling of self esteem. For deep down we know that the grade, even the wonderful A+, is an artificial construct that we experience given from the outside. The grade can be taken away as easily as it is given. The inner exaltation and self esteem of accomplishing excellence cannot be taken away at all. And this creates radiance: radiance of being, radiance of health and vitality. And this creates a wonderful rapport and relationship with one's self which always extends out to relationships with others as we are less defensive and more compassionate and confident when we feel well inside. When we experience this excellence we raise our standard, even if only once, and we will forever measure our future accomplishments by this standard until we raise the bar again. For from this experience we have created new neural networks in the brain which will be there for us to activate again. And through the repeated activation of these new networks we will strengthen them and the older networks of lesser excellence will fall away as we stop using them. In short, we will become addicted, through the familiarity and repetition, to the chemical rush of excellence, the rush of endorphins that feels so delicious.

WHAT BRAIN RESEARCH TELLS US

Our brains create intense chemical reactions, and our experiences of these chemicals are our feelings. We relate to these feelings as if they are permanent and unchangeable. Yet, in truth we have choice of which feelings we want to experience. Our reactions are ours, and no one can make us feel a certain way unless we choose to. As performers we learn very specifically how to change our feelings and tap into feelings we desire. We do this through intention. When we repeatedly use the same intention we strengthen that neural activity in the brain. Building a character on stage is the same process as building character off stage. It is, in short, the process of taking control, directing our thoughts, and our actions. When our thoughts and actions follow certain desired paths, we develop character. Our brains are our on board computers that allow us to develop in any direction we choose: towards becoming more fully who we are, following our natural developmental impulses, inclinations, and calls, or towards becoming what others want us to be, conforming to norms and standards set by other people. When we are brain washed we submit ourselves to forceful indoctrination of a fixed set of beliefs that destroy our basic convictions and attitudes. Our brain knows no such difference; it simply takes in the information and creates connections thereof. Only with a watchful, vigilant awareness of the vast power of persuasion that the media and corporatacracy indoctrinates us with daily, can we become masters of our own fate and resist the terrible pressure to conform. If we conform, we develop our brains more or less like everyone else and lose the opportunity to think for ourselves.

Our brains will be uniquely ours by developing them with independent thinking. Independent thinking and brain development require deep focus and concentration. Brain research shows that strong concentration and attention create deeper learning. The performing arts channel exactly this kind of focus, with one main difference from text book learning; performing requires movement and emotion. And kinetic movement and deep emotion deepen the learning process into long-term memory. For knowledge without experience is philosophy whereby knowledge coupled with experience becomes wisdom.

Performing arts cannot be learned from a book very effectively, even as it can be a supplemental form of learning. For real learning a studio is required and an expert instructor must impart the knowledge and offer the appropriate experience for the students to progress and develop. For the end result of performing is a bodyful experience not a mindful one. Yet, we have lost touch with our bodies in part because Descartes implored us to separate the body from mind in saying "I think therefore I am" and we bought into it. Even my computer spell-check acknowledges mindful as correct and bodyful as incorrect. Dr. Maria Montessori knew that to force children to sit in chairs to learn was a mistaken idea because she knew that movement created learning. Movement is the basis of life: stop moving...and die. Movement is mandatory for a child to develop fully. Through movement we discover our world. The performing arts begin with movement and doing. It cannot be passive, it must be active. And this is exactly how our brains develop. If our brain is passive it will degenerate and will not grow. Take the passivity out of your lives- stop sitting in classrooms and stop sitting in offices, stop watching TV, stop surfing the internet, stop the video games, stop the chat rooms and blogs, and see what happens. I encourage anyone who wants to grow to do this exercise for yourself and experience what life gives in return for your attention to it. The addiction to TV in our culture is a great example of uncritical thinking which facilitates groupthink. Turn your TV off and see how your life and thinking changes.

Neurons that fire together wire together, this is a basic axiom of brain activity. And neurons that fire together repeatedly create stronger neural networks. So be careful and pay attention to what you fire. In our performing work, we develop our ability to change ourselves actively. Our bodies, minds and spirits are our instrument to play and express with. We work with this instrument every day and discover the means to retrain our thinking. We use Brain Gym or Educational Kinesiology, meditation, intention, mental rehearsal, and deep emotional experiences to train and retrain ourselves. All of this kind of work is scientifically documented to create neural vitality, deeper learning and stimulate new brain activity. Beyond this science we embody and experience quantum principles in our ensemble training.

QUANTUM PRINCIPLES AND ENSEMBLE TRAINING

We live in a holographic universe where every cell contains the universe. Separate and isolate each cell and discover the universe inside. Divide each particle as far as you can and the whole is contained within. We are all connected in the whole and the artificial separation we have constructed is an illusion that tears at the fabric of our existence. In ensemble training we experience, viscerally, this truth. We become part of a whole in such an integrated way as to feel the fusion of our self with the group, with other individuals. The role of each player is egalitarian. There is no hierarchy, although admittedly a few students and many parents do not understand this way of thinking. Their brains are wired to see more lines as more power and more importance. This is embedded in our economic model of the more the better. It does not matter that more building and construction means less natural ecosystems and that eventually the end result of this thinking is that we will have no natural habitat for the thousands of species we share the planet with, of which we are but one minor species in a huge array of biodiversity on our tiny planet in our galaxy. And if we all want more lines in our plays we will destroy all the smaller lines that are integral to the whole of the play.

When we boil it down to the lowest common denominator we are all composed of the same thing and that thing is energy. Waves of energy, and when observed the very same wave energy becomes particle and mass. Energy is everything and everywhere. When we work with energy and become sensitive to it, verbal communication is less necessary to express what is already known. Performing work teaches this kind of awareness and sensitivity. We learn to shift our energies with the blink of an eye. We learn to express the energy of different character. We know that time is an illusion because we experience, if we are lucky, the timelessness of good performing. Physics shows that time does not exist as we know it, that in the whole is everything: past, present, and future. In our performing arts work we explore this concept and are privileged to see it, every once in a blue moon, until we understand it, through the synchronicities, synergies, premonitions and telepathic communication that ensemble members cultivate by working so closely together in trust. It is known that in this kind of collaborative environment our hearts entrain together, and our physiological processes fall in sync, like when the females begin to follow the same menstrual cycle. These are but a few of the gifts offered in ensemble training.

The riches of great stage work begin with ensemble interrelatedness and interaction, just as the quantum principles elucidate. Even a one person show will not exist unless it has an audience to make it real through the interface of interaction. It is the interrelatedness of partners working off each other and the reactions that ensue which create the fireworks that make a great performance. We do not sit in an isolated lonely chair by ourselves answering questions while learning. We are collaborating with other persons. We are gaining sensitivity and compassion towards others through the trust we work to develop in the process. We live and die together. We succeed or fail together. We are responsible to the whole through our individual actions. Just like the delicate balance of family life, finding just the right amount of individuality combined with sensitivity to other family members is a key to harmonious family life. This takes generosity.

Performing is an act of generosity. It is not the attitude of 'look at how great I am' which our TV shows along with many unknowing teachers and directors espouse. It is not the simple act of taking the stage with no prior training and performing to show off which High School Musical depicts. Performing is an offering of one's heart and soul to an audience. The development of this comes from training the instrument.

WHY TRAINING MATTERS

We have established that training one's instrument in the performing arts means being in a studio and with an expert teacher. It simply cannot happen from a book, an instructional video, or a computer. The live interaction is paramount to training. For training in this regard implies a person in the know instructing and coaching a novice towards the desired proficiency.

In a developing young person performing arts training offers an experience to engage all of one's senses and imagination and actively develop one's self by reaching beyond what one has already accomplished, delving deeper into the self, uncovering what lies beneath the awareness.

Training, through routine and repetition, develops a strong mind and body. The old Russian expression in ballet for instance, is "the first day you miss class you feel it, the second day you miss class everyone sees it". What they see is what everyone sees, that you are not as sharp or fit to master the class work after missing two days of class. And every dancer knows this truth. But why is this? Why is it required to practice so much and so hard to achieve becoming a performing artist? One answer lies in the extensive studies done about what makes the difference between being good at something or being great and achieving excellence. They data and results are surprising: it has nothing to do with talent and has everything to do with practice. The more practice put in the greater chance of achieving greatness. It is estimated that is takes ten thousand hours of practice to get to the level of expert. That is approximately twenty hours of practice every week for ten years. Or four hours of practice a day, if you take weekends off, for ten years straight. This takes unyielding commitment. To stay with an activity that long requires perseverance, dedication, concentration, endurance, love, talent, enthusiasm, sacrifice, awareness, and self-reliance. It offers all the highs and pitfalls of a long marriage. Complete with the vulnerability of being hurt in the process.

Hurts are bound to happen. And how valuable they are when they happen. To be wounded from a poor performance, an undesired casting role, a humiliation or embarrassment due to one's ignorance, etc, - all of these experiences offer chances of growth. For growth only happens through the discomfort of the unfamiliar and unknown. Often it brings pain. If we do not allow ourselves or our children the good fortune of staying with their pain and facing their fears, we have most certainly done a disservice to them. We have interrupted their development. So often I see adults and parents thinking they are helping a child or young person when in fact by making a choice for them. For instance, they are robbing them of the opportunity to practice decision making skills. Or by speaking to the teacher for them, they are enabling the child to be dependant. Or by giving into their hurts and taking them from the pain they are interrupting the natural process of growth. Or by buckling their seatbelt because it takes too long to let them figure it out themselves, they lose an opportunity to practice important motor skills. We have teenage kids now who do not know the most basic of skills of cleaning, cooking, etiquette, etc. that all teenagers are most certainly capable of. We have a new psychological term called post-adolescence to label those twenty and thirty somethings who still live at home. We have postponed adult self reliance into the twenties when it used to be that puberty signified a transition into adulthood. In training, we cannot baby our children: the challenges are too tough, and the sacrifices too extreme. The rewards of accomplishment means we have faced our fears alone, through introspection and making new choices. No one can do this for us. And we do it if and only when we are ready. Some folks are never ready. The younger one starts the more hard wired this process is in the brain. The more familiar it is and the less difficult it is each time we practice it.

The joy one discovers from training and accomplishing is ecstatic. Early training, if in a balanced life of wholeness, not the frantic overextended life, creates an orientation to life of joy and hard work. Training offers ecstasy, which is instinctive when one accomplishes great things like new growth. This is an inner journey taken alone, even as we work with others in the process. In fact, having others witness and support our accomplishments and inner joys validates our worthiness and lovability. This is a key component to ensemble training. We grow *together*, we laugh *together*, we scream *together*, we cry *together*, we fail *together*, we get up *together*, we argue *together*, and we love *together*.

HOW TRAINING IS FACILITATED

Now to get to this wonderful experience, there are prerequisites. First and foremost, there is attendance. One cannot gain anything if one isn't participating. Talent is second to attendance. Full participation must be offered to the work. There is no commitment when one knowingly misses the training. And it is a mistaken idea to think one can be dedicated to a genre, say theatre for example, and commit to five or six theatre programs all the while not being one hundred percent committed to any of them. If you do not make it a point to be available for your classes and in good health for each training session, you are not exercising full commitment. The great things you will gain from true commitment require you have those dreaded days of not wanting to attend class and not wanting to see your director. Sticking to something and overcoming hardships can only come if one is truly committed. To intentionally miss classes is to not know the depth of the work. Depth is only known through completeness and fullness, seeing and experiencing it all.

Once one is committed to full attendance, preparation for each and every class further facilitates training. In performing arts study there is work to be done outside class each and every day. If one fails to do this work one holds one's self back. To have the time and energy to do this outside homework one cannot be overextended. I have seen my best students fall by the wayside and lose leadership skills because they did not prepare for class or rehearsal. Their work takes on an air of mediocrity. What was once special is now average. And I have seen students with little talent demonstrate great preparation for their classes and succeed wonderfully. Training is facilitated when one is enthusiastic, committed, and healthy. Performers, like athletes, have a responsibility to maintain health. And we learn in our classes and training how to stay healthy. It is a vital part of the training in fact.

All of this work is terribly demanding, which I am sure you are seeing. It requires great vulnerability. And we haven't even touched on the deep emotional honesty that is necessary to do this work. Students who live in households with open, honest, and direct communication will have an advantage as they will be used to acknowledging their true feelings. Students will work with vulnerability when they are in an atmosphere of trust and support, and every training center must offer this. By trust and support I mean that the students trust they will be treated with dignity, even in the rough and tumultuous times of struggle and growth. And they will feel at all times the director is on their side, even as they are hearing a barrage of criticism. Students learn how to take notes, what we call criticism, without defensiveness. They learn that the notes are for their growth and not to be taken personally. This training facilitates maturity.

Where we do this work has a large impact on the work. A training facility must be professional in standards. Everyone has probably had the experience of walking into a building and instantly feeling that the facility is subpar. The work space should be considered a sacred place and should be treated accordingly.

Of course one of the most important aspects that facilitate training is the level of the director and faculty. How can you know who is an expert teacher or director? Find out the background and experience of the teacher. How many years of real life experience in the career has the teacher had? Going from learning in college to teaching is a sure dead end in the performing arts. First of all, many of the highest professionals do not consider college training very good. Colleges are interested in all the exterior rewards and motivations I have listed above. College training is chock full of teachers who have little professional experience or experiences in the lower levels of the profession (although this may be changing as more artists are taking up the secure positions colleges offer and the college programs are expanding rapidly – we will wait to see how it unfolds). And lastly, colleges are corporations that are part of the corporatacracy that breeds conformist ideals. I know many talented performers that have left colleges early, even prestigious institutions like Julliard because of their limited boxed-in attitudes that stifled the artistic instincts of the student.

Secondly, if one learns in college and goes right into teaching all one can teach is from the limited knowledge and experience one gained in one academic institution; which is not the same as learning from the experiences of working in the real world and gaining from the diversity and variety of other directors, choreographer, musical directors, teachers and cultures. Nothing can replace the training and learning from the real world experience.

Besides working in the real world, look to see how many years and what kinds of experiences does the teacher have in training students. Certainly a seasoned teacher will have more to offer than a green one. Also very important to look for: can the teacher demonstrate the material taught, especially if a young teacher. An older teacher must be able to impart the knowledge without always demonstrating.

Does the teacher have a proven track record of accomplishing their mission? This would be an indication of reliability.

Is the teacher open to discuss the work and answer questions with students and parents? Inevitably there are misunderstandings and miscommunications that are part of any relationship because we all filter our perception from our own unique neural networks which leads to different interpretations. So having a teacher that will explain him or herself and discuss the work is an indication of generosity and open mindedness.

Even after you look into all these area and find a teacher that fulfills these qualities, it is still a matter of chemistry. You must find the right teacher for you, and sometimes (for me always), intuition is the best source of knowing.

KNOW YOUR GOALS

In your training you must keep in mind your goals. You must revisit them and reevaluate them as you grow. Goals change and evolve. Staying true to your goals is paramount. Get to know your goals, and be careful not to have a goal to have something to fall back on. Performing is too demanding to try to prepare for another career as well. Medicine is a demanding and competitive career choice and many pre-med students do not make it. Yet we would never dream of asking a pre-med student to have something to fall back on.

Write out your immediate goals in the performing arts. Write your 1 year goals and then your 1-3 year goals. And write your further goals be they in college or career. Write other goals you have in other areas as well. Now under each goal write your resource for fulfilling those goals. See where your priorities are. If you are in a quandary about a decision to do one thing or another write out what advantages and disadvantages each choice would offer in regard to achieving your goals. Usually doing this will make the decision clear, not easier, but clear as to what is to be decided. The hard part of following through with your decision is part of your training.

If you want to perform in the school play, for example, and yet you want to perform at a training center like The Gate, do this exercise. I hear students wanting to do the school play because of social reasons, for social relationships. This is a wonderful reason to do a play in school. Yet it will not get you the training you need to compete in the larger arena of getting into the college of your choice. Also, do not neglect the relationship[s with your friends at the training center. In fact, they may be longer lived because of your common career goals and the deeper commitment you share with them to the work. Always ask yourself: what is the best way for me to achieve my goals. Performers who perform without training are at a distinct disadvantage to performers who train and also perform.

We help our students and children perform better when we allow them to be self-directed. This is the path to true development. Doing what others want of us, taking orders, pleasing others, are all ways to sabotage our own development. Young people learn responsibility by practicing being responsible. It is learned experientially, not conceptually. When kids are treated as adults they almost always rise to the occasion and act as adults.

When teenagers are working alongside adults, like they have for ninety-nine percent of the history of mankind, they cultivate adult tendencies and choices. When teens are only embedded in teen culture, they act like teenagers. The gifts of the multi-age learning environment are well documented and are demonstrated here at The Gate.

Children are natural learners. They only need a guide once in a while to jumpstart their work, or assist in the process. They do not need to be coerced into practice, attending classes, or any other facet of learning. All that accomplishes is taking the natural learning instincts out of them. Nothing can replace being really listened to and the feeling of worth a child feels when an adult heeds what is told to them by a child.

WHY YOUNG PEOPLE ARE SHORT-CHANGED
IN OUR CULTURE

Yet in our culture, children are discriminated by their age at every turn. Rarely can they practice the responsibility they desire and actually need to grow by. They are overwhelmed by the ever growing restrictions we place upon them. And they are over extended in their activities because we have not pointed out the ill effects of stress and instead have impressed upon them that they should be doing it all.

The corporatacracy aims their consumer strategy at young kids and robs them of their inner dreams as they become driven to be cool. The arts are not cool in our culture, sports are. The arts are made into competitions, we learn to dance to win, not to experience the joy of dance. We sing to win, not to enjoy the freedom of vocal and musical expression.

In our result driven culture, process becomes something to get through as fast and as easily as possible to get to the end – the joy of doing is unknown.

The arts are transformative because they offer experiences of irrational, demanding commitment. In this work we are trained to follow our impulses, be available for our partners, work off our partners, open our hearts and minds and every pore in the body, be specific, work in soft focus seeing nothing in particular and seeing everything, honor what others bring to the work through an enthusiastic "yes", listen to our bodies, let the work do us, plant seeds and work organically, allowing the creative process the time it needs to develop fully and naturally, be in the moment, develop character with our actions, and offer all of our work in a spirit of generosity.

Life is to be lived in ecstasy and the arts are a door in. Children embody the secret of our nature and are our best teachers. The dark material that is inevitably part of growing is to be celebrated and valued. There is no right or wrong, good or bad, it is all an illusion we have created through dualistic thinking and dividing up what is whole. The child is indeed the father of the man, as Dr. Maria Montessori pointed out.

The Banker Kings

A look back at the Good Ol' Days

When we think of good ol' Kingdoms we think of a ruling power that has no checks and balances, of rulers who make the law, change the law, and are always above the law, logically. Kings can do what they please, to whomever they please, whenever they desire. Their only fear is revolution of the populous.

One person revolting is easy enough to squelch. Dissenters can be made criminal. Torture can be applied. But if the populous as a whole rises up and revolts the king is in trouble. Serious trouble.

So the king is smart and conspires with his underlings to maintain control. Secrets held from the populous keep the populous unaware of truth. Giving the populous goodies, be it money, gifts, property, whatever, keeps the populous appreciative and subservient.

Saying one thing in public, all the while saying another thing behind closed doors, controls the populous' thoughts to be regurgitated official king-driven thoughts.

Of course the old strategy of divide and conquer is easy to do by pretending to let the people think they have their fair say, let them make teams, and let them fight it out, keeping them distracted and feeling important. King-driven education will insure the children grow to be good citizens, as defined by the king, and lead each successive generation toward hard wired brains rife with conformist minds.

Allegiance to the king grows with every protection the king offers. Threats of king violence against the wrong doers convinces most people to remain obedient. The few who dare rebel are hung in front of the populous; everyone points the finger and declares how bad the renegade is. The all go home, flip on the screen of distraction, count their blessings and all are none the worse off for their unintelligence.

But...if the king did not control the money supply of his land he was beholden to his bankers. Once the bankers charged the king interest for their loans, the king was a debtor. This is why *"Give me control of a nation's money and I care not who makes the laws"* was stated by Mayer Amschel Rothschild. In one swift brush stroke the king becomes underling to the banker.

Behind the scenes the banker calls the shots and while the king still appears to have power he now has strings attached to his livelihood. The bankers make decisions, deciding how they want the king to act, and the king agrees, all in secret. And all in the populous are none the worse off for their ignorance. The king is now a puppet and the bankers control the strings.

Of course the bankers want nothing more than to maintain their stranglehold on the king and therefore the populous. Best way to do that? Create a war, which will distract the king and keep him busy while his resources deplete, which means he has to go back to the banker for more money, and more debt.

Better yet? Play both sides of the war, finance each leader and control both while they both are busy proving their might. When the war is finished, finance the reconstructions and rebuilding and own both lands while amassing greater wealth.

Mark Ruhala| Collected Critical Essays

Even better yet? How about a war that never ends? Say a war on terror? A war that must be waged for the protection of the populous, because god knows the populous would be dust without the king's powerful and expensive military to protect them.

Oh, no real terror? Create some. Easy to do when you finance both the freedom fighters and the terrorists. Then fear monger the populous into believing the propaganda, give them more goodies, threaten them with treachery if they disagree, and re-educate them about what it means to be a good citizen. And...

The hoax is complete. The only thing that would change the power structure is a financial crisis where the banks are insolvent, right? Wrong...the king bails out the banks saying they are too valuable to lose, while convincing the people to fear the dire consequences of chaos and anarchy if the banks go down. The people gladly submit, wipe their brow with a sigh of relief and thank the king for his wisdom and action.

The king reiterates he is a king dedicated to Main Street and that is why he is using the Main Streeters' money to save the banks. The king laughs on the way to the bank as he feels his renewed power to negotiate with the banks because he just saved them.

The people go back to their screens and watch the beautiful princesses sing and dance, or they go to the coliseum and watch fight night.

The bankers regroup and know they must do better next time, for the absolute worst thing that could happen would be a revolution. And revolutions can only happen when people think enough to want change, a better life. Of course the logical step is to stop the people from thinking.

Best way? Drug them.

Oh, not openly, but secretly, and filled with propaganda that the drugs are "good for you".

How about in the water supply? Everyone drinks. And maybe the food, everyone eats too.

Oh, sure, the air too. Sick people can't muster energy to revolt.

Excellent! Finance the drug makers, on both sides, i.e. the legal and the illegal, and watch the populous run to the doctor.

And even better? Finance the doctors and offer the people insurance for their sickness but call it health insurance.

Now the populous is very busy working to make a wage to pay for: their taxes, their lost income to bail out the banks, their doctors and insurance costs, and mostly, their interest on their debts which comes from the easy credit the banks gave them to get them into debt in the first place, which caused the financial crises, but which made the bankers untold treasures of money in the process.

Wow! Thank god we don't have kingdoms anymore!

Honest Holistic Scientific Health Care Re-form

Care of health nature-ally

Care of health has been idiotically skewed toward a perverse idol worship of the modern medicine man, the *DOCTOR*. No longer a personal experience and responsibility, care of health is now intimately involved with the cold steel of an industry awash in self-interest, greed, corruption, and hidden agendas. No end is in sight for the ills of modern man; we don't even pretend to see an end game, for the industry perpetuates the game to extremes of which the vicious cycle of health care hurts the one it aims to heal. The public at large is hoodwinked into the dogma of the official line and people, or shall we say patients, dare not cross that line for fear of the doctor's wrath. We turn our keys of power over to the doctors and breath a sigh of relief as we abdicate personal responsibility and accountability knowing of course that the "expert" is now in charge and will tell us what to do.

What he tells us to do will focus on the symptom and will not address the root cause. What to do will be dosed or surgical or will be terminal, or may contain all three. What to do will not aim at prevention. And why should it? In our capitalistic system the doctor is a money maker like everyone else and abides by the rules: make profit, make more profit than the next guy, for this is your right and your privilege. In this system, if the doctor heals the patient and no longer needs to treat him, then the status of his career diminishes. He no longer is making his largest profits, he no longer has a waiting list of patients-to-be, and he no longer will be able to compete with other medicine men. In this system to keep the patient in health does not pay. Hence, massive multitudes of sick people accruing astronomical medical bills firing the kiln of interconnected health care costs until the oven overheats and nothing whole is made nor left.

Health care reform as we know it has two main goals: one, to get each and every individual insured, and two, to reduce costs. Let's *really* look into and investigate these goals which seem so noble and worthy on the face of it. Since, in the view espoused here, the latter will make the former goal shift into a new focus through our investigation, let's deal with the money side, costs, first in this discussion.

The question to ponder, to dream about, to look deeply in and around, thinking as absolutely open-mindedly as possible is: how do we lower health care costs? If we only look at our current ways, our present system of health care, we limit ourselves, box ourselves in and will not discover if there are other ways to approach health care. Perhaps our system itself is the root cause of the escalating and exorbitant costs of health care. Unless we ponder all our imaginations can come up with, we will lack the creative fortitude to re-form.

So, how *do* we lower health care costs? Why do health care costs reach such expensive levels that employees and employers cannot afford them?

Health care is designed overwhelmingly by the "experts": doctors, politicians and health care business executives. It is not difficult to see that these "experts" depend on each other for their livelihoods. The incestuous policy making of these experts has been written about and studied enough for me to need not extrapolate or cite here. Short to say there is a conflict of interest in the very same experts who create health care policy! This root problem must be changed to re-form.

How do we create a health care system that will not reflect the author's need to make profits and get elected and reelected? How do we create health care that has a ring of truth to it – to care for the health of the people? In our current system, the expert's inherent conflict of interest cannot be avoided. It is how our politicians get elected and legislation for the doctors and the industry executives get written and made into law. So where do we turn? Universities? They too are part of the incestuous club of back scratchers. This too has been shown and need not be taken up here. Lay persons? Would they know enough, have enough knowledge to make intelligent decisions? Doubtful. And might they also have self interest as a primary motivator?

Well what about a consortium of all the above? Would a balanced group of individuals from varying sectors of society provide checks to the conflict of interests inherent in this group?

Perhaps we need to explore letting society make its own health care policy; a true free market industry where the market demand creates the product without the interference from government regulations. Do not dismiss an idea such as this simply because it is not of present thinking or ways. Look very deeply into it, map out the path of this hypothetical re-formation and like a good chess player anticipate the moves as far out as you can see. Often what seems at first as immediately reckless and destructive, will turn out efficient, safe, and extremely productive and constructive after the initial birthing and growing pains have subsided.

People in a free market *act*. People in a spoon-fed regulated government market *listen* and *obey* and *give up their power*. Our government regulated market has helped make our citizens fat and unhealthy, sick and lazy. Our government food pyramid has been shown a fallacy, our medical cures do not exist even after billions of research dollars, the drugs we are prescribed hurt and kill us and the foods we eat are regulated to be poisoned and modified which makes us unhealthy. The air, water and land we breathe, drink and eat from, are poisoned and dying from the food industry, among others. We are fed TV screens twenty four hours a day everywhere which ask to be used and watched and we listen, watch and get "entertained", give up our independent thinking as we are radiated while watching advertisements which convince us that health is found outside ourselves. Reform what is on our screens and reform the masses.

How about creating a federal campaign- if we have to have government involved, to educate the masses to think independently and to discover the vast wealth of health to be found outside our current health care system and motivate people to be responsible for their own health. Of course this is a pipe dream that would ruin the profits of the status quo which government is a part of. *Even still*, if we put all our money into this kind of campaign it *would* work and re-form.

The true cost reduction and savings in health care is barely mentioned in this current cyclical debate. Nothing would reduce costs more than not needing these services because the population is healthy and *well*. Of course this would ruin corporate profits and would not be tolerated let alone considered!

Begin to educate five year olds in kindergarten and carry on throughout their years in school. If we must have schools why not have healthy schools? Why do we have such unhealthy cafeterias complete with food that is toxic and environments that are toxic and a paradigm of manmade chemical toxic living? We can create a generation of healthy people if we attempt to and see the *long view*.

Meanwhile we can give sick people in hospitals HEALTH food and educate them about healthier ways of eating and living. How about a new philosophy of parenting which fosters, supports and values breast feeding as the best start of a healthy life? Even better, how about the huge savings on giving birth responsibilities back to the mother and women and keep the birthing in the home where costs are cheap and the environment actually boosts the immunity of the new born? When we have a population of individuals taking responsibility for their health we will finally eliminate the root cause of health care spiraling costs: unhealthy people using the system way too much!

Yet let me remind readers that a health care system without unhealthy people is an industry failure in our business model! No profits can be made without need or demand. An entire industry would need to create new jobs. Of course the logical shift would be towards a well-care industry: caring for well people just like the well baby visit to the doctor.

People would now turn to the *well-care industry* for maintenance just like they do with their cars. We schedule our car visits precisely so we do not wait until the car breaks down to get it fixed. We wash it and make sure it gets good gas and good oil to burn daily. We keep tires rotated and replaced and we change out filters and belts. In short, we maintain the machine so it will not break down. If we neglect this maintenance we suffer the consequences.

Now the key with our car's maintenance is that we do not treat one part while hurting the other. We would never tolerate our mechanic damaging the hood while working on the engine. Nor would we allow the transmission to be hurt while we fix the radiator. Or break the windshield wipers while fixing the headlights or radio. Yet this absurdity is exactly what we do with our bodies. We destroy our lungs while treating our hearts! We poison and destroy our livers while treating joint and muscle aches and pains and headaches! We go psychotic while fixing our depression! Ad infinitum...all drugs have side effects that hurt us. This means escalating health care costs and it must end to bring costs down.

If we must spend tax dollars, let the government spend on a national juicing, fasting and a raw food program, organic only, that would motivate people to participate by offering free health care for those who achieve optimal health: optimal weight, optimal blood work levels, optimal cardio fitness, optimal strength and stretch, optimal mental health and fitness, etc. THIS IS S NO BRAINER WIN/WIN EQUATION! Once people are in optimal health, free health care is giving almost nothing away, it costs nothing! When folks are healthy, like myself, we can easily go without health care because we do not need it nor use it as I haven't for twenty five years. How much savings is that? Oh, add into that all the savings of my two sons, ages four and eight, having never had a hospital stay, never receiving vaccinations, having no need for a doctor and never had insurance. Yet both are as healthy as can be.

Meanwhile as the unhealthy work in the government program toward optimal health they will learn first hand, through experience, the drug free approach to a healthy lifestyle and body. We would rid ourselves of all kinds of ill conditions like allergies, asthma, auto-immune dis-eases, cancers, heart dis-ease, and more.

People would learn that our bodies are a system *based in health* through balance of energies, proper PH levels, interrelated equilibrium of regeneration agencies and the proper balance of mental perspectives that keep us stress free.

If, as is clearly shown, *ninety five percent of our health care is from stress related conditions*, then we must address this primarily and most stringently.

We know the stressors- they have been documented. Now think how they not only cause health care costs to rise, think how they also lower productivity in the work place and cause extreme depletion of resources and profits. Perhaps that will motivate us to change our ways if nothing else.

If all of this seems too easy and logical that is because it is. It is easy to find studies on the multitudes of stressors that keep us unhealthy, from physical to environmental to mental. Our health care debate ought to be directed towards the elimination of these stressors that cause the ninety five percent of all ill health conditions! To do less is to foolery.

The studies on drug free approaches to health care are abundant, from homeopathy to chiropractics, to acupuncture, meditation, organic raw whole foods, juicing, fasting, raw food diets, hands on healing, prayer, dance, yoga, etc.

Once these ideas are debated and actions are taken and we create a healthy population, health care costs will be extremely low and our desire to have each and every individual covered will be easy due to the rare need for health care and insurance thereof.

A final warning: these health care reforms will eventually be so effective that the population will need to fill the vacuum that doctor, hospital and pharmacy visits consume us with now.

To avoid this dilemma keep the health care debate focused on its current list of concerns that do not even pretend to get to the root cause but only encourage the reorganizations and rearrangements of the systems that presently keep us unhealthy.

Art and Competition
What is Gained and What is Lost?

In order to investigate the ramifications of Art and Competition we need first agree on a definition of each.

In this essay the word art is meant to be interchangeable with self-expression. The word art comes from the Latin *ars* which means skill, originating in the Greek work *techne*. Practicing an "art" is developing a specific skill. That skill is "the art of". Once that skill is practically used to create something we have a "work of art." The "work of art" is always based in self-expression.

In this essay the word competition implies an activity that sorts winners from losers. To compete is always meant to aim to be superior over someone or something. One can compete with a computer just as one can compete with another person or team. A competitor must always have an opposition of which to compete against, even if said competitor is one's self. To compete with one's self is to aim to better one's self to beat and be superior to the earlier self that set the standard that is now in competition.

Based on these meanings above if we mix competition and art we are essentially mixing self-expression with winning and losing. An apparent dichotomy immediately presents itself; how do we judge the self-expression as a winner or a loser? What is the quantitative criterion for the judgment? Can it be anything but subjective?

The Lay Person as Judge

In many instances the winners are chosen by the public, of which no necessary education or knowledge of the art is required to judge. The obvious mediocrity of that kind of competition where the "lay" public is judging is nearly impossible to refute (unless one argues that the public is replete with experts in said art, which is untrue in today's society in any art form). If the judges of a competition have no special training, education or knowledge of the art they are judging, they are basing their judgments on something other than the skill (of which we have determined that they know little or nothing of) of the art. Inherently this kind of competition is mediocre at best.

Now what happens to the art form and its place in the culture when the public determines who is best, who is superior? It would seem obvious that the standard of what is superior would be set by the uneducated (in this art) public, thereby making the winners an arbitrary category judged by irrelevant criteria regarding the art form. In this way the public would be making their own value system of the art form which has little or nothing to do with the history of the art, the fundamentals of the art, the nuances and subtleties of the art, or any studied or actual experience knowledge of the art. Contrasted with the judgment of a knowledgeable person in the art, a teacher or professor, a mentor or educator, a trained expert or specialist, the "lay" public's opinion will be less informed. The end result of this kind of competition is the watering down, or dumbing down of the art. It has to be such, for as the public continues to make decisions of winners based on irrelevant and arbitrary criteria, those entering these kinds of competitive contests will be looking toward the criteria of the judges who decide the winners to set their practice habits. If the judges deem a specific trait is a winner in spite of the fact that the "experts" in the art deem that same trait an obstacle to achievement, the competitors would be foolish not to listen to the judges and ignore the experts, if they plan to compete earnestly. This entire way of competing in the arts is clearly destined to break down and break up the art as is currently known. Unless there is a strong base where the art is still practiced with the integrity of its lineage, the cultural changes of the art, the watering down of the art, will be made manifest.

There is no moral judgment in this assessment as we are interested here in investigating into the ramifications of competitions and art and not judging the ramifications. For in the end, all art forms are man-made, and are expressions of humans. Art, if anything, imitates nature. Nature is established, art is conceived.

The Experts judging Art Competitions

A different kind of competition in the arts is a contest where the judges are the "experts" of some kind, be they teachers, professors, practicing professional artists or specialists. In this kind of competition the artist is judged more for the skills learned from her teachers of the art. In this way there will be inherently more integrity to the contest. For short of having clearly set criteria of unmistakable winning guidelines, such as in most athletic events, these kinds of contests are decided by subjective personal means. So if the judges are "experts" there will likely be more integrity, unless the expert judges set aside their integrity and judge by preferential, subjective means.

In athletic competitions where one wins by a set rule, such as scoring the most points, winners are automatic and unbeatable (one can always debate the calls of officials or umpires, but points are points and not debatable). In athletic competitions where judges determine the winners, such as skating or gymnastics, "experts" are always used to judge, and as above, these judges can use their integrity of judging or use preferential, subjective means thereby infecting the integrity of the decisions. In our present investigation into competition and art, this kind of competition with judges from the field, known as experts, is our concern.

Now in this kind of competition, if the criteria are clear and the performers know the criteria by which they will be judged, there will be less arbitrary winners. For example if one is singing in this competition, and say one of the criteria is that the performer sustain a musical note for a certain length of time, and the performer does so, then she has clearly executed that said skill. However, when judging the quality of the sustained note, we still get back to a subjective opinion from the judge. In hockey a goal is a goal, in basketball a score is a score, in football a touchdown is a touchdown, - no matter how pretty or ugly the points were made, they still count, no subjective opinion counts, only the points count. But in judging an art there will always be a subjective aspect of the judging because the judges have to determine non-definite criteria like quality and style, without a set quantitative rulebook to judge.

So even if the art competition is judged by the "experts" of the field, it is always going to be subjective by nature. Now what happens when artists are judged by opinions rather than actual undisputed points scored or the undisputed checkmate? One difference is that rather than honing the skills for the game or match one may hone the skills for the judges. Particular judges like particular qualities so one focuses on those aspects rather than the fundamentals of the art. As the judge becomes highly important rather than the scoreboard, the relationship with the judge becomes a relevant issue. One may spend time cultivating that relationship rather than doing the work. Rather than everyone having the same chance as in a scored competitive game, in this regard each competitor does not necessarily have the same chance. Now reputation, personality, attitude, appearance, etc. will all become relevant. In short, the artist relying on self-expression only will suffer if not taking the other side issues seriously. Hence the subjective judging adds more superficiality to the art than the pure self expression.

Artists as Winners and Losers

Competitions create winners and losers. In the arts, everyone is a winner in that they have created something from nothing of their own doing, and that is life-affirming by nature. Isn't the point of creating to express? Isn't the artist who creates a winner for doing so… even if his art work is unrefined or unskilled? Isn't the inner life of that person better off for the insight and fortitude and openness to create? Art therapy is a valid experience because the arts help us to know ourselves better, to express and release our inner life, be it aches and angst or joys and bliss. Every creative act is a winning activity. To make an artist feel second rate, or worse, like a loser, is antithetical to the arts. The arts are uplifting and developmental. They require hard work and dedication, courage and stamina, and they build character in the process.

What the Artist Gains in Competition

So what is gained for the artist in the arts competitions? One gains experience performing, experiences of losing and winning, experiences of failure or success, traveling around to new places, making new friends and meeting new people, artists, teachers, etc, becoming better known, perhaps a celebrity star. Yet all of these gains can be gotten without competition. One can always gain performing experience, and in the process experience the success and failures that are natural and a part of the art, which teach one how to handle the winning feeling and the losing feeling of defeat. Performance groups travel and one can meet new friends and contacts. Festivals are a great way for artists to group together and meet new people and show their work without competition, although competition has snuck into the festivals today as well. It is not that competition in the arts is wrong or bad, it is a matter of looking into the issue to see what really happens, what the real repercussions are of artists competing and to see if there are other ways that would better serve the arts. If artists agree there are better ways than we ought to do something about this.

What the Artist Loses in Competition

A lot is at stake for an artist when competing. The artist can lose face, can possibly fail mercilessly in front of peers and judges, can spiral down into extreme self-doubt, can experience ridicule and intimidation, can injure themselves emotionally from any number of hurtful experiences while competing. All of these things can happen as well without competitions but the competition raises the stakes and the added pressure can be debilitating. To be catapulted from no one to instantly stand in front of thousands or millions of viewers is an experience that can overwhelm and undercut the confidence of an artist who has not paid their dues and are essentially unprepared for this kind of leap. What we can say is that every time an artist puts herself in a competition she is placing a desire to win at the forefront of her psyche. A desire to win has little or nothing to do with creating art. When in fact we create our art in order to win something we will always stray from the authentic experience of creating our art for the sake of self-expression. Even if the art was created in an authentic process born of the organic impulse to create a self-expressed piece, once it is put into a competition the piece no longer carries the purity of the original and is now placed in the realm of gaining the right judgment to win the contest. In the process the piece is not valued for what it is, in and of itself, but now is valued as a winner or loser. It is easier to learn to be a good loser when you just did not score enough points rather than someone judging you inferior to another. The former is objective and unarguable; the latter is subjective and arbitrary. It seems there really is quite a bit at stake here in arts competitions. And it seems the costs are rather high in terms of creative manipulation away from the authentic artistic experience when we bring competition into the mix. Perhaps it is time for artists to stand up and begin a collective conversation of critical thinking regarding the ill effects of competitions in the arts and on artists and make changes pursuant to that dialogue's outcome. For every winner in the arts competition there are hundreds, and at times thousands of times more losers that are created by the contest. Do the benefits for one or two or three top winners justify the damning effects of losing on the multitudes who began in earnest at the beginning of the contest?

Intimidation – the Psyche Out

A well known aspect of competition is getting into you opponents' head, and to psyche her out. Those who succeed at getting into the head of their opponent and intimidating them have a clear advantage. The psyched out competitor will never perform her best. If the goal is to win then the use of this intimidating strategy is an integral part of the competition. And the age old strategy of divide and conquer will always bring advantages to those who understand and can execute this strategy. A team divided is a team functioning poorly: get into the heads of your opponents and get them frustrated and get them to take it out on each other and watch your advantage grow. To be nice and not use this strategy is a ridiculous strategy if winning is your goal. Competition, like business, places being nice second to the ultimate goal, to win, to make profits. If niceness is an obstacle to success eliminate it. If niceness is your priority over winning, suffer the disadvantage with your good heart. Artists are already sensitive people and prone to insecurities, for the art forms require the artist to lay themselves out there bare for all to see, and that is scary. Intimidating another artist is not hard if that is one's goal. And if winning is the goal then intimidating the opponent is a useful strategy. But I ask you, why the heck would we want to put an artist in that kind of position? Again, it appears antithetical to the arts.

Where we are now

What is the end result of the plethora of art competitions today? All children grow up now with an indelible idea that competition is a natural and vital part of the human condition and experience. Survival of the fittest is based in competition, the sperm race to the egg is about competition, the school ladder is a climb through competition with one's classmates and peers from around the region and country, business is successful through best competitive practices, the dominant cultural entertainment is the highly competitive world of sports with a second place to the games shows, reality shows, award shows, performing competition shows, ad infinitum. From this early conditioning, children succeed or fail in relationship to their competitive skills. They strive to find their rightful place where they are a winner, be it on the soccer field, in the orchestra, in math, or as a cheerleader, they are all looking for a place to succeed which means outcompeting the others in that field. At some point they are taught that Charles Darwin completed some brilliant scientific work that shows us how life works and that life is driven by a competitive engine that runs on self interest and looking out for number one. In short, we cut our teeth in competitions and we cut our winners and losers from the same cloth. We create losers. We make certain persons losers. We deem the winners to be superior over the rest. We divide our children as winners and losers. We separate our children as winners and losers and offer the winners greater opportunities and further privilege. The losers we leave behind. The losers become those that watch the winners. The world is and becomes a ruthless never ending series of competitions starting with the toddler beauty contests and little league competitions all the way up the ladder. If you are a winner early, good for you, you have it made. If you are a loser early, good luck! In the end the bottom line result is a separation and division of the community.

Another paradigm

What if we kept competition where it truly naturally fits and serves human beings – in games and sports where only the points count, the finish line is crossed, the furthest throw wins, the highest jump takes all, the winning hand trumps, the knock-out punch TKO's, the pin is executed, the fastest guy is tops, and the checkmate is irrefutable? Competition has vast merits in these games and sports and in a balanced world where competition is a part of rather than the whole, these kinds of competitions will be highly valuable through the character they develop without the stripping of the self. And for those who choose not to be a competitor they will have alternatives like the arts.

What if we keep the arts as recognition of self-expression without need for judgment – the actor delving into the human condition, the singer transporting us into musical realms, the dancer defying gravity and human limitation, the sculptor showing us a new way to see, the photographer who captures the magical image, the pianist who's lightning speed and accuracy leave us gasping, the novice finding an authentic voice, the raw talent of a new creator? What if children knew they could participate in the arts and be acknowledged for what they create, what they express, without any further need to improve or compete, just for the sake of it? If there are no competitions the point of it would be to just do it. To do something for the love of it, really just because you love doing it, is the most sublimely irrational thing we can do. Just like the irrational and mysterious process of falling in love, where we do not do it for ulterior motives we do it just because it is coming out of us and we feel it and it feels really good. It sends floods of confidence and self worth and we feel more capable than ever… just because we are in love. We didn't decide this it just happened. Just like real art. It just happens. We don't decide what to do we just do it. The novel we thought we were going to write turns out to be totally different because it wrote itself. The dance we thought we were choreographing becomes a wholly different piece because it came out of us that way. When we sat down to play that wonderful piano piece we were transported to a very different time and space because we just got into it without any need to go anywhere other than the playing. Following our impulses creates the most individual works of art. To be recognized for this kind of work is to be validated for being who we are. The artist needs no outside validation; the work created is validation enough, if we raise our children on this kind of paradigm. The outside validation is icing on the cake, you might say, or it can also be looked at as an interference with our natural self-reliant and self-validating potential. In either case the child or artist who creates out of his own imagination and impulses and receives acknowledgment for this individual work experiences something extremely different from the artist who is looking to win and does so.

The Artistic Expression

To express one's self in an artistic way is to create something original, coming from the individual's unique perspective and orientation to their life experience. Like falling in love, it is something that happens to us, it is not driven by our desire. Just as we may desire to fall in love, we cannot make it happen. Falling in love is a feeling that is involuntary; any forcing of that feeling is an inauthentic and phony experience that is manipulated into existence. The same is true for artistic creativity: just because we want to write a novel or write a song, or paint a painting or sculpt a statue, we can no easier make it happen than we can fall in love at will. We can put ourselves in a position that will help facilitate that experience, we can go out to meet people if we want to fall in love, or we can begin to dabble with our artistic instruments and play, but we must wait for the natural innate impulse to overcome us before we can create anything artistic. Otherwise we have created something from our head, from our conscious driven mind, from our thought process; that is not the same thing as our intuition and imagination. The novel or song that writes itself is an authentic experience and work of creativity. The novel or song that is written without inspiration, only from the conscious mind is a novel from a different origin. There is nothing wrong or bad about this kind of work, we are simply drawing a distinction between the two kinds of creative artistic work. Often artists must create on a deadline, or create when little or no inspiration is felt. Yet any artist who knows the experience of having the work come through them, from an inspired space, from an intuitive energy, where they are the vehicle for the work to manifest itself rather than the creative source, will know this distinction we are talking of here. Just as the person who has been swept off their feet and experienced the falling in love rush of chemicals of well being and heightened happiness, knows the distinction from the experience of talking one's self into the feeling of falling in love or projecting that feeling onto the other. In this way the truest impulse to create an artistic work is about opening to be moved by the invisible, organic, mystical, and mysterious process that propels one into the state of losing one's self in the work, where individual awareness is secondary to the heightened consciousness of an expanded mind, where time and space are altered from our physical understanding and we have unlimited access to creativity. In other simple terms it is the same experience of the athlete in competition transcending into "the zone": that place where physical reality shifts and the athlete experiences time and space so differently that they can make every shot, do the perfect routine, swim faster and more effortlessly than ever before, know beforehand where the ball is going, execute the jump or technical athletic move with exceptional ease and grace and execution, etc. - where the feats are moving through them and are not consciously felt as "making it happen". The classic sports analogy is when the great athlete is at the end of the competition and they are so tired that natural instinct takes over, where their minds are out of the way and they just rely on instinct.

The Body's Wisdom and the Artist

When we get our minds out of the way and are able to rely on that "instinct", be it the "killer instinct" of the athlete or the "creative instinct" of the artist the body becomes the source of our work. The body has an innate wisdom: it was developed long before the mind, the brain as we know it is a recent evolutionary development. The body is as old as the earliest forms of cells uniting. The body solved duality by having the whole be made of complimentary halves. The body has a dominant side and a weaker side naturally, an acidic and an alkaline balance naturally, a regenerative capability and a killer immune system naturally, a right brain left brain distinction naturally. The body reflects the natural laws of equilibrium and balance by uniting the dualistic aspects into an organic whole. When we transcend our minds and allow instinctive, intuitive energies to move us we are much more in touch with our primal, original impulses which are built on the creative forces of propagation. Without this force, what we will call "propagation", the species would not continue. The body and it trillions of cells desire to propagate and move into the future and create a continuum of life. Life affirming attributes contribute to this instinct, and creating is the origin. To create a work of art is an extension of this inclination and desire to move forward and propagate. Our minds could care less about this. Our minds may have no regard at all for this. Our minds may deceive us in ways the body is absolutely unable to. The body carries truth of experience and cannot alter or manipulate the actual experience. Our minds are very clever at disguising our experiences into what we want them to be. Our minds can even block out experiences from awareness. The brain is aware of only thousands of bits of information per second but our bodies take in the millions of bits of information we receive every second and retain it. When we connect with the bodies' truth we are accessing a richer, vaster reality and truth. The arts are better served when originating from the body and the "field" our bodies perceive from. That field is the electro-magnetic energy that holds it all together, that is the glue of life which prevents everything being in a constant state of entropy. Life builds on complexity. Through more and more complex forms we organize and improve our functionality. The arts are best served when creating organizing memes of unity and insight and investigation. Competition has other agendas. Those agendas are very valuable, in their proper place, and without dominating the entire spectrum of human behavior. Competition is a glorious test of will and endurance and smarts and prowess. Art is a sublime experience of the creative instinct.

"Self-control is twice as important as intelligence

in predicting academic achievement."

THE GIFT OF

SELF-CONTROL

SOME COMMON SENSE GUIDES TO RAISING SUCCESSFUL CHILDREN

&

THE DEVELOPMENT OF RUHALA LEARNING

Please, while reading this essay, place the stress on the first syllable in the words "**self**-control". While unnatural and foreign it will vigilantly remind us that self means not under other's control; only one possible kind of control here: *self.*

"In any culture, the development of self-control is crucial. This ability, which depends on the prefrontal cortex, provides the basis for mental flexibility, social skills and discipline. It predicts success in education, career and marriage. Indeed, childhood self-control is twice as important as intelligence in predicting academic achievement. Conversely, poor self-control in elementary school increases the risk of adult financial difficulties, criminal behavior, single parenthood and drug dependence," so states Sandra Aamodt, a former editor in chief of Nature Neuroscience, and Sam Wang, an associate professor of molecular biology and neuroscience at Princeton. Sandra and Sam are the authors of

Welcome to Your Child's Brain: How the Mind Grows From Conception to College.

Ms. Aamodt and Mr. Wang will be quoted in this essay extensively from an op-ed piece they wrote in the New York Times, February 19, 2012. [*UNLESS OTHERWISE REFERENCED, ALL QUOTES BELOW ARE FROM THIS OP-ED PIECE.*]

Here is the link to the full article: **http://www.nytimes.com/2012/02/19/opinion/sunday/building-self-control-the-american-way.html?src=me&ref=general**

Mark Ruhala began teaching children full-time in 1988 and founded his own learning center Mark Ruhala Studio in 1991, which transformed into the Broadway Training Center in 1996 and is still serving the children and youth of Westchester, New York today. In 2004 Ruhala founded The Gate: Gateway to the Arts through Transformational Energy, which transformed into the Ruhala Center. Throughout this quarter century Ruhala has expanded upon his original teaching philosophy of "theatre as a vehicle for personal development" and created Ruhala Learning: a method aiming for *optimal* learning and development. Ruhala Learning has been greatly influenced by educational author John Holt (*How Children Fail, Learning All the Time*) and his common sense philosophy: "...the human animal is a learning animal; we like to learn; we are good at it. What kills the processes are the people interfering with it or trying to regulate it or control it." Also author and award winning teacher John Taylor Gatto has been an inspiration to Ruhala Learning with his extensive writing and lecturing based on a simple idea "When you take the free will out of education, that turns it into schooling." — **John Taylor Gatto**

What follows is a breakdown of the scientific opinions provided by Aamodt and Wang, provided in italic "quotes", a hyphen and A&W, then the connections to the Ruhala Learning model which follows.

"Like many brain capacities, self-control can be built through practice." - A&W. What is wonderful is that science is now catching up with common sense. Mothers and care givers have known throughout history that how a child is raised makes a significant difference. Yet, in the past few decades we have been directed by doctors to believe that our brains need drugs to overcome their inborn deficits; that our DNA is so hard-wired that we really have little say past what we are born with. Ruhala has been critical of the bio-pharmological psychiatric pushing of drugs on children which are mostly untested or under tested at best. Ruhala agrees with Dr. Peter Breggin, author of *The War Against Children*, "Because children are among our most vulnerable and treasured citizens, we especially need to protect them from psychiatric diagnoses and drugs. We need to offer them the family life, education and moral and spiritual guidance that will help them to fulfill their potential as children and adults." The environment a child lives in is much more the cause of brain deficits than inborn chemical imbalances. Ruhala Learning works to make changes in the child's synaptic brain firing by creating healthy habits and practices through learning self-control.

"Fortunately for American parents, psychologists find that children can learn self-control without externally imposed pressure. Behavior is powerfully shaped not only by parents or teachers but also by

children themselves. The key is to harness the child's own drives for play, social interaction and other rewards. Enjoyable activities elicit dopamine release to enhance learning, while reducing the secretion of stress hormones, which can impede learning and increase anxiety, sometimes for years." – A&W. We can go even further and remind ourselves of the many scientific studies which have shown that when a mother and newborn child do not immediately meet at the breast seconds after birth, overwhelming stress overcomes both. The result being that the mother's emotional, physical, and psychic expectation to nurse her child, as women have been doing for thousands of years in a natural continuum, and the child's same ontological expectation, are not fulfilled and the most important moment for oxytocin, well known as the "love" hormone, to fill the pair with bliss is lost forever. All children are gifted a huge advantage to begin their lives with the mother love and bonding that comes from womb-to-breast intimacy.

Ruhala's own children were born at home in natural drug-free child birth aiming to begin their children's lives with little secretion of stress hormones and maximal secretion of "love" hormones. Ms. Celina Ruhala, Ruhala's wife, aided herself by retraining her brain patterns and thought conditioning with a beautiful therapist who used hypnotherapy to undo the old ideas about childbirth pain and fear, replacing them with fresh insights and healthier ideas. Childbirth is a human's first orientation to life outside the womb. It can be filled with the unnatural sterile environment accompanied by many "expert" strangers who are trained to medicate and have little trust in the innate wisdom of the human body and the mother's instinct. Or birthing can be ease-filled with loved ones close to assist, a water source to allow the mother and baby to relax, home-cooked nutrition, the comfort and privacy of home, and a midwife who is not an "expert" but *is* expert at letting a mother birth her baby and to intervene if and only when necessary. Why do we exactly begin our children's lives in the inherent stress of a hospital where an expecting mother is treated like a patient, a sick person?

Ruhala Learning is based in child-driven learning, the most stress-free learning available: it is built on the idea that children develop by using their brains and that there is a significant difference in how the brain functions when *following orders* as opposed to *leading oneself*. John Taylor Gatto urges us "… to examine in your own mind the assumptions which must lay behind using the police power to insist that once-sovereign spirits have no choice but to submit to being schooled by strangers." The stress of schools is responsible for many childhood perversions. Children rarely want strangers to order them what to do with the threat of punishment. What costs do children pay to acclimate and make this absurdity okay?

If the key is to "harness the child's own drive for play…" then we must recognize that coercing our children to do what we want them to do can be very stressful for them, while letting them do what they want can elicit valuable dopamine to enhance learning. This is not a recipe to allow children total freedom; rather it is a guide that Ruhala Learning follows. Teaching children who are doing what they want requires much less effort and gets much more results. This is evident to anyone who teaches children. Most often, the self-directed child in the midst of their chosen activity needs little intervention at all. They figure out for themselves what they need to learn. In many Ruhala classrooms children need little from the instructor other than to get out of the way and witness the self motivated learning that is taking place. Actually a scary proposition for teachers of traditional models that are taught they must *teach* the child for it to learn anything.

"Young children build self-control through elaborate, imaginative games like pretending to be a doctor or a fireman." – A&W. Theatre games, a major tool of Ruhala Learning, are a direct link to the "elaborate and imaginative games" which build self-control. Perhaps this is why so many children would rather play theatre games in a creative acting class than actually learn skills and gain knowledge about acting by listening to the teacher. Over the years it has taken Ruhala time to realize why children desire this so, as he too would rather "teach" them what he knows and what he knows they need to know to become an actor. In fact they are teaching themselves when they are playing the games Ruhala facilitates – this was what he learned. But as a "teacher" he felt like he was doing nothing when he let them simply keep playing without intervening. But the reality is, as Ruhala finally learned, they are learning in the absolute optimal way: through first-hand, direct experience without any teacher. As John Holt articulated so clearly, "the most important thing any teacher has to learn, not to be learned in any school of education I ever heard of, can be expressed in seven words: Learning is not the product of teaching. Learning is the product of the activity of learners."

After the school day is over, children seem to need to balance all the left brain coerced behavior and learning by letting loose, which actually translates to freeing themselves to do what they want: to be impulsive. Coming to Ruhala theatre classes after school they do not lean towards "learning" because they love the improvisational exercises so much; so much so that they could play these games all year long without ever doing any other theatre exercises. In these games they are experiencing Ruhala Learning: completely self-directed, relating to each other with full focus and participation, giving and taking easily, listening and reacting effortlessly, fully engaged in the imaginary circumstances, living out fantasy after fantasy. What could be more fun?! And now, get this, the experts are telling us that studies show this is the *best* way towards self-control which will breed success for their futures!

"Frequent practice is crucial. Montessori preschool instruction, which has been shown to lead to strong academic achievement, incorporates self-control into daily activities." – A&W. Dr. Maria Montessori knew, over a hundred years ago, that self-control is one of the most desirable qualities in children and she based her entire program upon this principle as its foundation. To walk into a true Montessori classroom is to enter a freedom room: children of many ages all together freely doing what they want within the confines of the activities and structure presented to them. The room is filled with the silent whispers of people busy at work in-joying themselves. Montessori believed so strongly in the self-determination of the child that she advocated putting their mattress on the floor and allowing the child to decide when it would sleep and when it would wake. As much as that would alleviate the stress children often feel in going to bed at a certain hour, the stress would transfer over to the parents who would have little idea how to trust this radical proposition! And yet the self-regulation that Dr. Montessori advocates innately teaches the young person to listen to and trust their bodies, which is essential for self-control.

Given this scientific validation of Montessori education Ruhala wonders what stops the Department of Education from at least integrating this proven model into public education. Why, with all the talk of educational reform over the past few decades in this country, hasn't there been any integration of alternative models of education which have proven effective -models like Montessori, Steiner's Waldorf model, the Sudbury Valley school, Summerhill, or any of the many models that have already established themselves as hallmarks of good education, which now include the internet programs such as Khan Academy? This simple question begs research, and when one does the research one discovers that the Department of Education is motivated by an idea that children are to become the next workers in the marketplace and therefore ought not be more than order-takers; not critical thinkers who might disrupt the status quo. This serves the industrial/business/corporate/military needs of the powers that be and keep a class of peoples ready to submit to the poor and often inhumane workplace environment. Just researching the realities of how text books are prepared and marketed is enough to show one how business-driven is the backbone of education. It is not driven by higher ideals of empowering and enabling our young people toward self-discovery, liberal open-mindedness, critical reasoning, creative thinking, and a free-flow of give-and-take with others that leads to a community of learners who share (which is not cheating in the "real world" but is considered so in school) and develop bonds of common interest which reside in a peaceful heart. Ruhala Learning chooses the latter motivation. Again John Holt: "Education...now seems to me perhaps the most authoritarian and dangerous of all the social inventions of mankind. It is the deepest foundation of the modern slave state, in which most people feel themselves to be nothing but producers, consumers, spectators, and 'fans,' driven more and more in all parts of their lives, by greed, envy, and fear. My concern is not to improve 'education' but to do away with it, to end the ugly and antihuman business of people-shaping and to allow and help people shape themselves." Mr. Holt saw with his students, as Ruhala has seen all too often himself with his own students, that the dominating emotion of students is fear-fear of being wrong, of being laughed at, made fun of, bullied, not being good enough, not pleasing teachers and parents, not being popular, let alone the fear of getting in trouble by doing what one wants and not conforming. In a recent autobiography, the fine and accomplished American actor John Lithgow describes The Stockbridge School, one of many schools he attended in his itinerant youth, because it struck him so differently than others… "This was not your typical New England prep school, full of children of great wealth and patrician breeding. Oh no. With its renegade faculty and its raffish student body, The Stockbridge School was just the opposite. Its kids were roughly divided into two groups. Half were lefty New Yorkers, many of them Jewish and many of them children of divorce. The other half was a polyglot mix of foreign students, in keeping with Hans Maeder's international mission (the United Nations flag flew alongside Old Glory at the school's entrance). An ultra-liberal, ultra-casual atmosphere prevailed. Dress codes were non-existent. Every teacher was called by his or her first name. Folk ballads and union songs filled the air. The eighty-plus students were made to feel part of a huge, mutually supportive family, in many cases replacing the fractured families they had left behind. The school shut down many years ago, unable to survive after the messianic Hans departed the scene. But while it lasted, it was an artsy, outdoorsy, gloriously anarchic mess of a place…". Mr.

Lithgow goes on to admit that the day he graduated Harvard university, years later, with honors, that he felt he had gotten away with murder – he never finished any reading assignments, not one, and he created an independent-study program of which he never once opened the book but passed none-the-less! This is exactly what schools create: false, phony government-sanctioned learning that offers a degree that one can take and get a job with when little or no learning actually took place. Another student of Ruhala's, after graduating from Harvard, said she didn't learn anything there. Far from the exception, this is the ubiquitous message Ruhala hears from students continuously. Who are we kidding? Is this self-control or is this coerced conformism that breeds another actor in the workplace who has yet to figure out they are not fulfilling their potential?

"Aerobic exercise, which increases prefrontal cortex activity, is another way to build cognitive flexibility. Further benefits may come from Asian practices that require sustained attention and disciplined action, like martial arts, yoga and meditation. Though parents often worry that physical education takes time away from the classroom, an analysis of multiple studies instead found strong evidence that physical activity improved academic performance." – A&W. Anyone who has taken a break from their studies to go enjoy some exercise or sport knows that upon return to the study, rejuvenation and refreshment accompany one back. Hence, a renewed sense of confidence and vitality to wrestle with the difficulties of one's subject matter. The "further benefits" obtained by "disciplined" practices of martial arts, yoga, and meditation have been woven into the Ruhala Learning model for decades. The Ruhala Learning extension reaches farther with Brain Gym, Heart-Centered

meditation, the 5 Rhythm Wave dancing of Gabrielle Roth, already mentioned theatre games and Improv, and the precepts of Holistic Health and Fitness which Ruhala has been developing over the years.

Critical in this Ruhala Learning model is discipline – which is another way of speaking about self-control. Although some students and families may criticize the Ruhala Learning model for a perceived harshness and coarseness around its edges, this is really a misunderstanding that Ruhala insists on self-management and self-control as a prerequisite to being in the classroom. When it is not present, Ruhala philosophy asks for intervention from the instructor to implement this foundation of real learning. Implementation is never enjoyable for the out-of-control child and is therefore often misunderstood and construed to be punishment. With Ruhala's philosophy that a classroom is a community and a team that works together, the intervention is done in an open and public way, just as is praise, to reinforce the fact that we are responsible to our peers and teammates in the classroom. In this way the team is driven by open, clear purpose which all share equally, and support one another thereof. But today's protocol in schools insists that "problems" in the classroom be dealt with one-on-one in a private way which separates the behavior from the context and eliminates the possibility of shared learning and support from teammates, along with open accountability. Ruhala Ensemble programs have been successful over the years precisely because the team is built and strengthened in the open with group consciousness.

"The connection between self-control and social skills seems to be a two-way street. Helping children to identify their emotions and think through possible consequences before reacting improves self-

control, in the classroom and at home." – A&W. The arts are based in self expression and therefore inherently assist one in "identifying (their) emotion" by releasing it and not pushing it down and suppressing one's feelings. Vigilant to the idea that a classroom is a team, social skills are practiced in each and every moment, as children learn to listen and react to one another as teammates and not seen as competitors who stand in the way of one's succeeding to the top. When the goal is for the team to reach the top, no child is left behind. Ruhala learning is infused in these principles and creates memorable performances lighted by the invisible threads of team mentality. The group makes each individual stronger and makes each actor seem more talented than they are in fact – what a wonderful way to be supported by your team! When a team wins all the players are stars, not just the great players, but even good and the mediocre players. Ruhala will take a team chock full of good players who know how to play together with purpose over a team with great players who play individualistically. Any day.

"Children do not benefit from routine empty praise, like the cries of "Good job!" that ring out over American playgrounds." – A&W. Ruhala classrooms are notorious for having direct, critical language that can seem utterly insensitive. Yet those on the team "get" the reasoning and motivation behind the "notes" being given and learn to understand none of it is intended to be taken personally. Children become young professionals and learn the objectivity of hearing criticism without personal reaction – and they love it when they do get it because they feel liberated from their personal reactions and not controlled by them. They in fact practice self-control in this way and feel good within themselves from the trusted structure. When praise is in fact heard, the children know its

truth as it resonates with what is actually going on in the class work and not "empty". Ruhala has been driven by the idea that self-esteem is born through accomplishment and not other-directed praise. Therefore work ethic is taught and soon the child understands that through work the greatest reward is inner self-satisfaction. Too often parents and teachers, with loving intention, shower so much praise that the child is unintentionally hurt by it because it does not support reality. The day the child sees the true reality, the child is thwarted. Children know truth; they feel it instinctively in their bodies. And although they may come to override that intuitive sense with coerced pressures, the truth remains in their bodies. That makes it vital for children to work with body workers, chiropractors, acupuncturists, masseuses, cranial-sacral therapists, etc.. – this is a very overlooked aspect of children's health and much unneeded suffering occurs thereof.

"More effective is to praise a child for effort. "You're so smart!" doesn't suggest what to do next time; "Wow, you kept working on that math problem until you got it right!" carries a clear message about the desired behavior. Communicating high but achievable expectations confers tools for real success — the best route to true self-esteem." – A&W. Ruhala Learning uses clear communication about both desired and undesired behaviors. The group, team setting makes the communication even clearer as it is witnessed and heard by all and can be reinforced by the group. "Communicating high but achievable expectations" does "confer tools for real success" but doesn't go far enough unless the methods for achieving those expectations are clear and realistic. "When I communicate my expectation that a child actor face front toward the audience and they continually do not do so, I must look

at my communication and see where I have not communicated the method for the actor to do so," Ruhala states. "It seems easy and natural to me to face front, and it would be easy to blame the child for 'not getting it', but when I in fact find the way to get them to understand HOW to face front and act, I realize the problem was in my deficient communication and not with the 'slow' student. As my voice teacher used to say, it is never the student's fault, it is my fault if the student isn't getting it. And one of my dance teachers used to say she could make a stone dance, " Ruhala finished. Serious teachers hold themselves responsible for a student's success. High expectations for the student simply reflect the teachers own expectation. As the old adage says: to see the character of the person look to the fruits of his labor.

"An internally motivated approach to building self-control plays to traditional American strengths. Being self-motivated may lead to other positive long-term consequences as well, like independence of thought and willingness to speak out." – A&W. The grave danger and scary proposition today is that when children have "independence of thought" and a "willingness to speak out", these "American strengths" become a source of trouble making and are not respected with the sense of liberty they once were. To succeed today is to conform more strictly than ever to the norms imposed by the authorities of school, government, and the police/military. Ruhala Learning adheres dearly to the original American patriotic value of individual liberty. Yet it is couched in the "team" thinking that keeps the individuality in check by maintaining accountability to the whole, the group, the team. Balance is struck and accord is reached and community is served. The last place to look for self-motivation is in schools. Even the driven kids, the over achievers,

the gifted students, they all are motivated by an outside force be it parents, bribes, school rewards or punishments, etc...To prove the point, simply imagine taking away the rewards and punishments of schools and imagine what would occur. I imagine the students would be lost and it would take some time to reorient themselves to what real learning is – a self-driven journey for the fun and joy and wonder of it.

Just recently, in March 2012, a Council on Foreign Relations Independent Task Force report states that American public education is a threat to national security - (**http://www.cfr.org/united-states/us-education-reform-national-security/p27618**). Also in March, President Obama quietly signed into law The National Defense Resources Preparedness Executive Order -

(http://www.whitehouse.gov/the-press-office/2012/03/16/executive-order-national-defense-resources-preparedness) which allows the president and the Secretary of each Department to seize control of all resources including property, labor, food and water, et.al. even during peacetime. The stage is set, for anyone who wishes to see and connect the dots, such as the passage of so many laws like HR 347 (**http://www.gpo.gov/fdsys/pkg/BILLS-112hr347enr/pdf/BILLS-112hr347enr.pdf**) that restrict people from protesting, that we are in a dire situation of losing any real liberty and freedom as Americans.

"Helping your children learn to manage themselves, rather than rely on external orders, could pay big dividends in adulthood. With a little luck, they may end up agreeing with the legendarily hard-

striving Thomas Edison: "I think work is the world's greatest fun." –
A&W. The farthest reaches of Ruhala Learning takes from the rich American tradition of independent, self-directed, libertarian education; unschooling, as proposed by the great independent thinker John Holt. Mr. Holt stated, "I want to make clear that I don't see homeschooling as some kind of answer to badness of schools. I think that the home is the proper base for exploration of the world which we call learning or education. Home would be the best base no matter how good the schools were." Ruhala Learning has also been very influenced by author John Taylor Gatto who after decades of teaching and winning the Teacher of the Year Award in New York advocated that kids leave school to be home-schooled. "I've noticed a fascinating phenomenon in my thirty years of teaching: schools and schooling are increasingly irrelevant to the great enterprises of the planet. No one believes anymore that scientists are trained in science classes or politicians in civics classes or poets in English classes. The truth is that schools don't really teach anything except how to obey orders. This is a great mystery to me because thousands of humane, caring people work in schools as teachers and aides and administrators, but the abstract logic of the institution overwhelms their individual contributions. Although teachers do care and do work very, very hard, the institution is psychopathic -- it has no conscience. It rings a bell and the young man in the middle of writing a poem must close his notebook and move to a different cell where he must memorize that humans and monkeys derive from a common ancestor."
— **John Taylor Gatto**, ***Dumbing Us Down: The Hidden Curriculum of Compulsory Education***

As parents, Celina and Mark Ruhala desire to help their children "learn to mange themselves" because they too believe their children will be payed "big dividends in adulthood" thereof. So their children learn in a self-directed way without any set curriculum other than the guiding principles outlined above and a strong sense of love of reading, which will make one literate enough to learn anything one desires to. Having never had a reading lesson in his life, son Jordan finished all seven of the Harry Potter books in two months, totally driven by his own desire, as a nine year old. He was just assessed by a professional to be reading at high-school level at ten years old. Even though he is not being fed a diet of forced social studies, history, or other academic exercises, he will always be able to learn what he wants because his reading is excellent and his self desire is high. Whatever he does read he retains, unlike most of us that go to school – we learn to forget the material as soon as the test is over so we can move on to the next short-term memory exercise that will be tested. An example of this reality can illuminate: Mr. Ruhala was offering his son Thomas a lesson in fire safety and asked him what makes fire burn. He said air; his brother said more specifically oxygen and then went on to tell us that air has 78% nitrogen, 21% oxygen and 1% water vapor and other stuff. Ruhala was impressed and later that night told his students in a musical theatre class. They all immediately said that he was wrong that there isn't that much nitrogen. Ruhala had them look it up on their iphones. They were wrong, Jordan was right. They were high-school and college students and graduates, Jordan ten. Jordan is not special or gifted; Jordan has simply had experiences that allow him to learn on his own, all by himself. All children can do this if given the gift. All children are smart, bright, intuitive, and able. The most despicable aspect of schools is that we allow children to fail. No child ought to ever fail. In reality, as noted above, teachers fail, not students. Unfortunately we look the other way.

Ruhala's childrens' health is maintained through *self-managed* diet (food issues are not created), daily exercise (the basics: push-ups, sit-ups, and squats), brain exercises (Brain Gym and lots of math), with knowledge of homeopathic medicine (they ask for the medicine by name), hands-on-healing (Reiki, which they have learned from their own care) , chiropractic medicine (they love Dr. Dory and ask for her when their bodies are out of alignment), herbal medicine (they know the herbs they need to alkalize), and gardening (a favorite family pastime). They cook for themselves, do their own laundry, clean house, tend the garden, and assist in every activity their parents undertake. The boys play organized sports and learn more excellent social skills while being part of a team. They learn about sportsmanship and the spirit of competition- healthy competition. They grow and live in the world they will be adults in – not in a homogenized, age-divided, one-size-fits-all approach that must be conformed to. They are taught about the real world that they will have to live in as adults and understand the choices they will need to make when the time comes. They know what they will need to accomplish to get into a fine university program as home schoolers, should they desire to. It is a constant solo path because there is almost no validation of this lifestyle. But this is also a source of strength that reminds them to have "backbone", "thick skin" and a "strong sense of character" – all traditional patriotic American values. "Character on and off the stage" has been the Ruhala Learning way since 1991.

Ruhala thinks if we can re-claim children as the magical, self-learning, imaginative, self-regulating, creative, intuitive, resourceful, stress-free, vibrant and radiant beings they are, ...anyone can. It just takes will. And it involves thinking traditionally American values of self determination and liberty to live and let live. Neither Ruhala is a college graduate. Both are autodidacts and serious thinking people. All people are. All that is necessary is will. Ruhala doesn't believe he is special, nor his wife, nor his children. All human beings are special. And all are part of the intricate and interwoven web of humanity that is errantly placed at the center of the eco-system while it actually belongs somewhere on the periphery, in its right order. When we recognize the true station of human beings is a rather primitive one, compared to the vast unknown, the innate humbling quality of the experience allows one to think openly towards more cooperative and interconnected ways; which is, in fact, our true nature. Charles Darwin placed a much greater emphasis on cooperation as our true nature rather than competition. But those who popularized his work, including Aldous Huxley, were determined to stress competition. And to explore the reasons for that would be another paper altogether, save to say that our educational and parenting experts have, and always have had, agendas to serve which do not always allow for truthfulness. Yet common sense tells us that without cooperation as a very strong piece of human nature, human beings would never have survived.

The gift of self-control illustrates that one can think for herself and see through the double-speak, group-think, official conditioning of mass media and education and discover, if fortunate, that in fact "love is all we need". Imagine...

Mr. Ruhala is available for lectures, seminars and workshops.
He can be contacted at: mcruhala@msn.com
Also visit him at: **www.RuhalaCenter.com**

www.ingramcontent.com/pod-product-compliance
Lightning Source LLC
Chambersburg PA
CBHW070813290526
45795CB00002B/702